ALEF BET

TRACING AND PRACTICE

HEBREW WRITING WORKBOOK

Script

TRACING AND PRACTICE WRITING OF ALEF BET HEBREW CHARACTERS

THIS BOOK BELONGS TO:

_____

TIPS

Use pencil to practice directly on paper
so you can erase any mistakes.

Tear out pages and insert into
plastic protector sleeves,
then use thin white dry erase markers
to practice over and over again.

THE ALEF-BET LETTERS

ה	ג	ל	ב	א
hay	daled	gimmel	bet	aleph

י	ט	ח	ז	ו
yud	tes	chet	zayin	vov

ס	נ	מ	ל	כ
samach	nun	mem	lamed	chof

ר	ק	צ	פ	ע
raish	kuf	tzadik	pay	ayin

	ת	ש		
	tof	shin		

ץ	ף	ן	ם	ך
final tzadik	final pay	final nun	final mem	final chof

watermelon

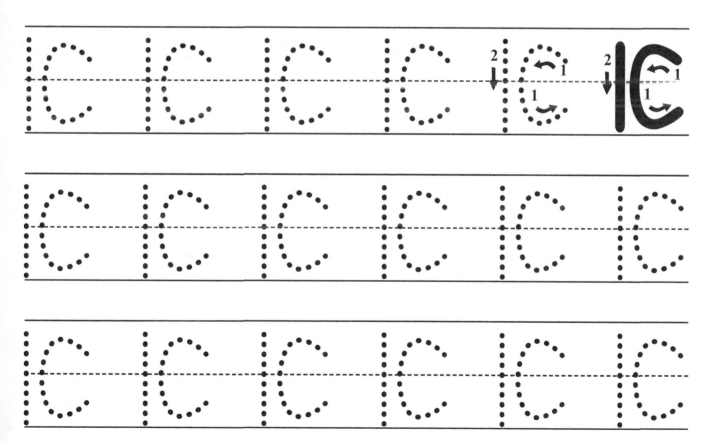

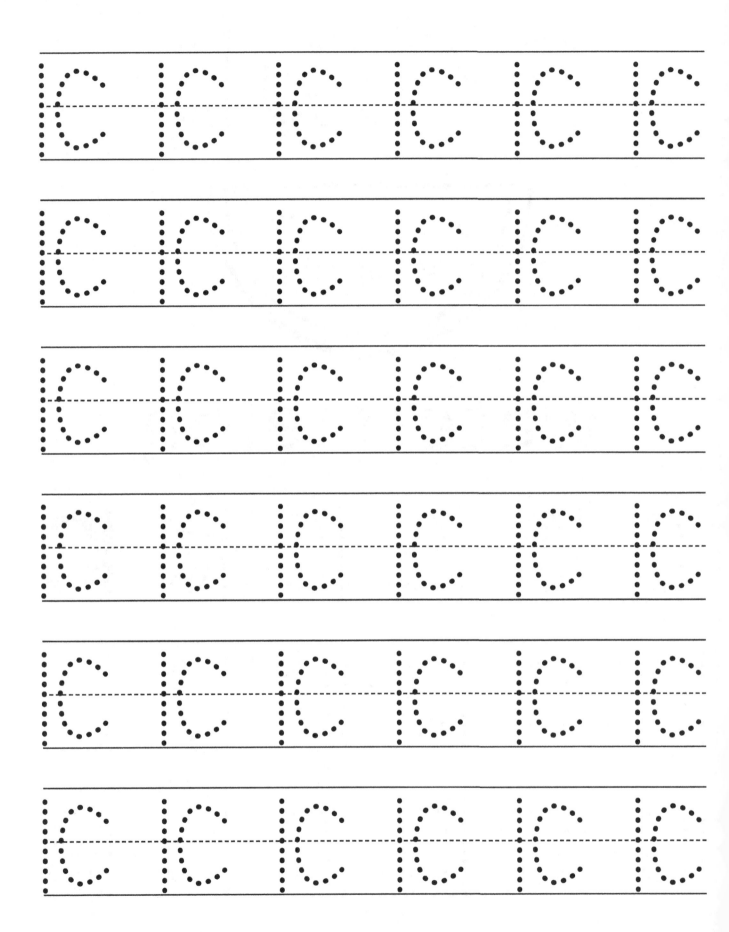

banana

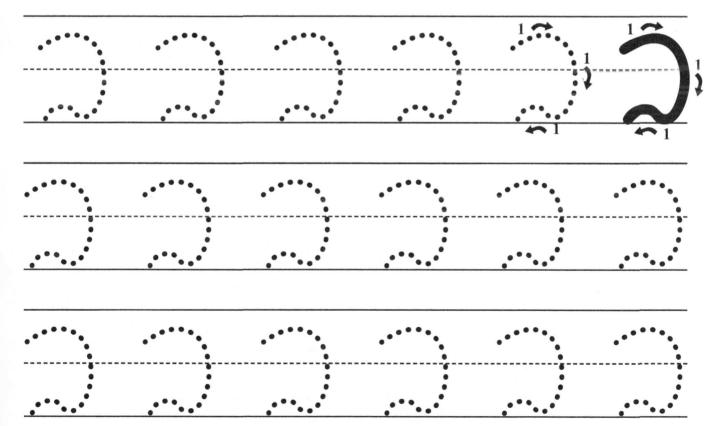

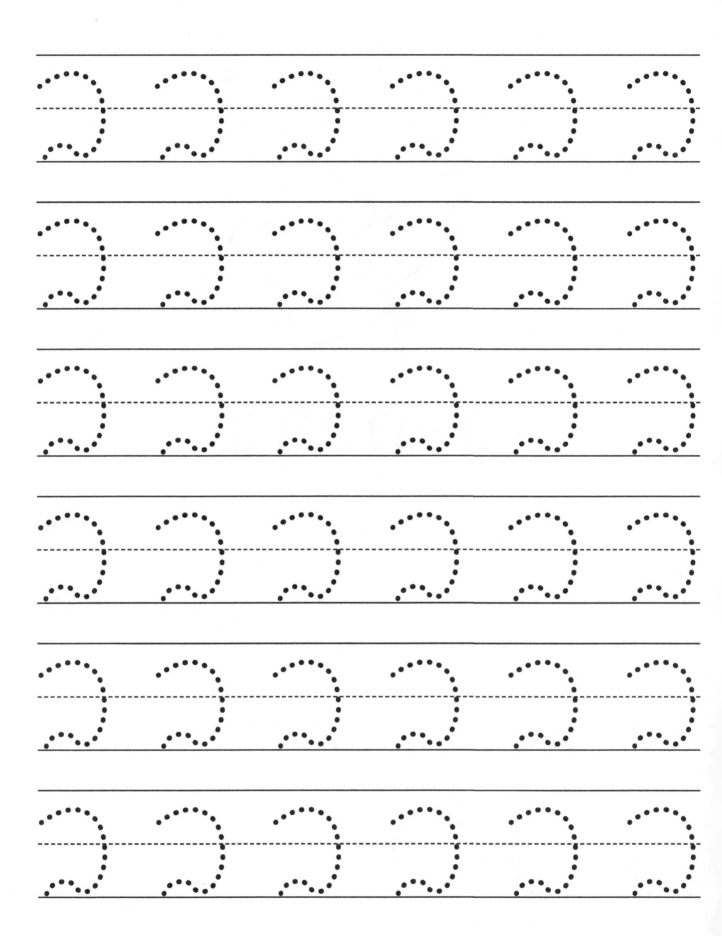

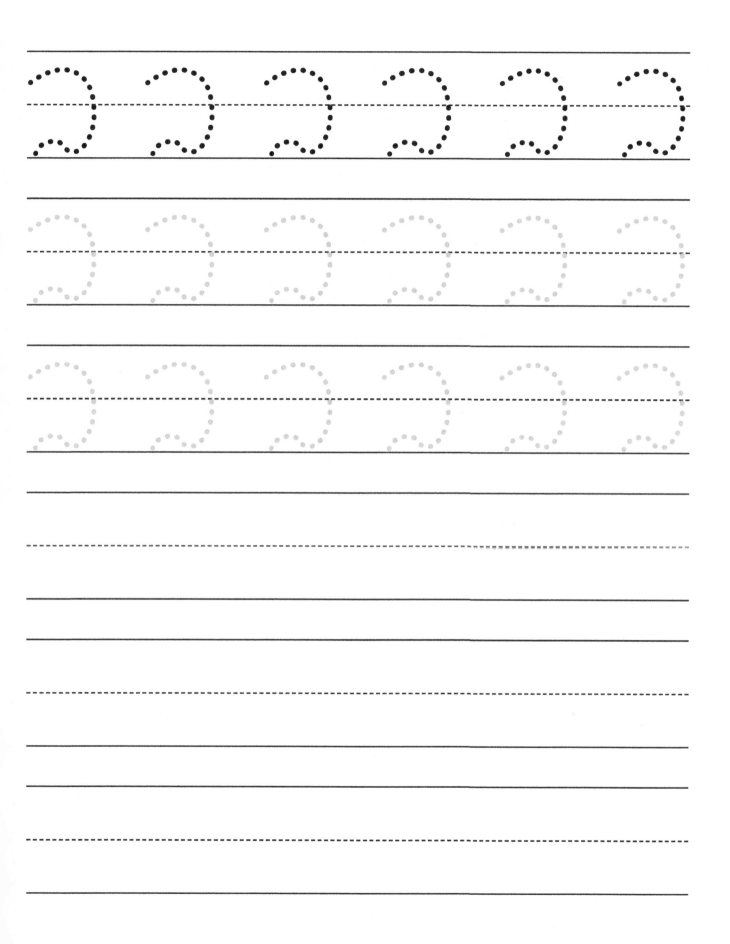

ice cream

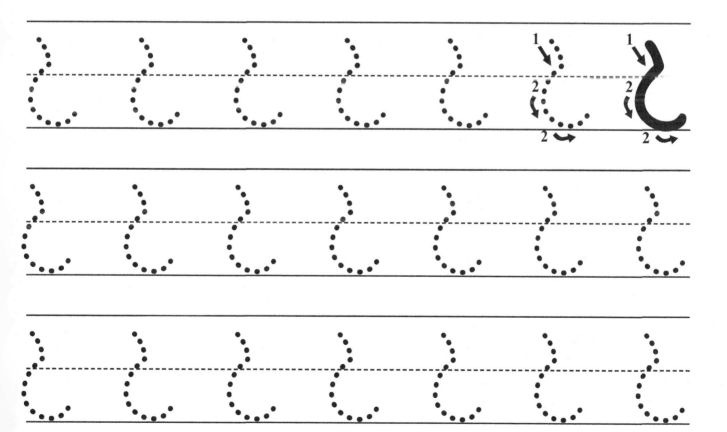

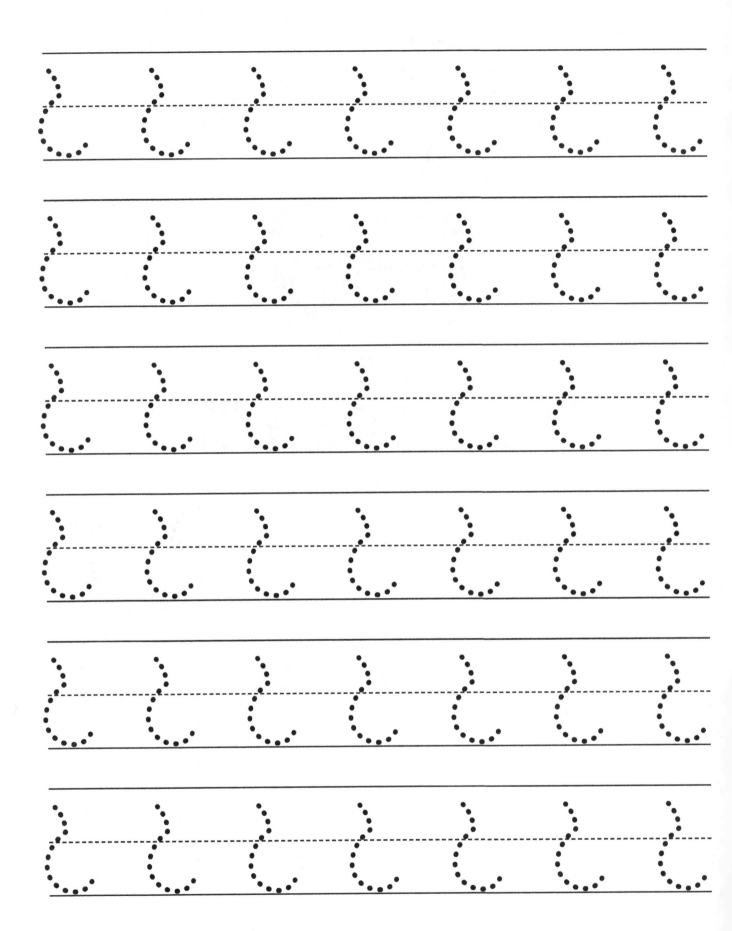

bee

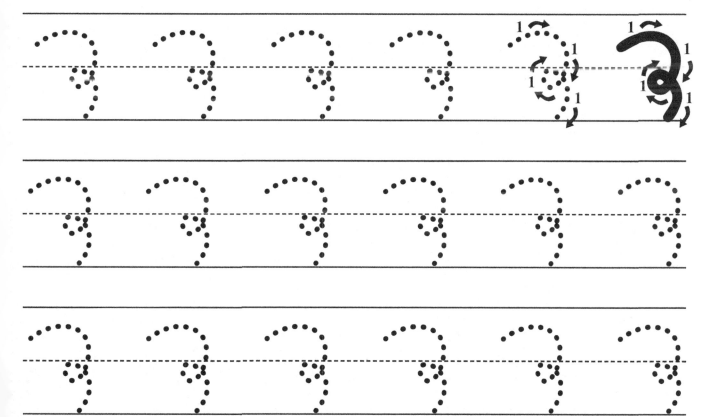

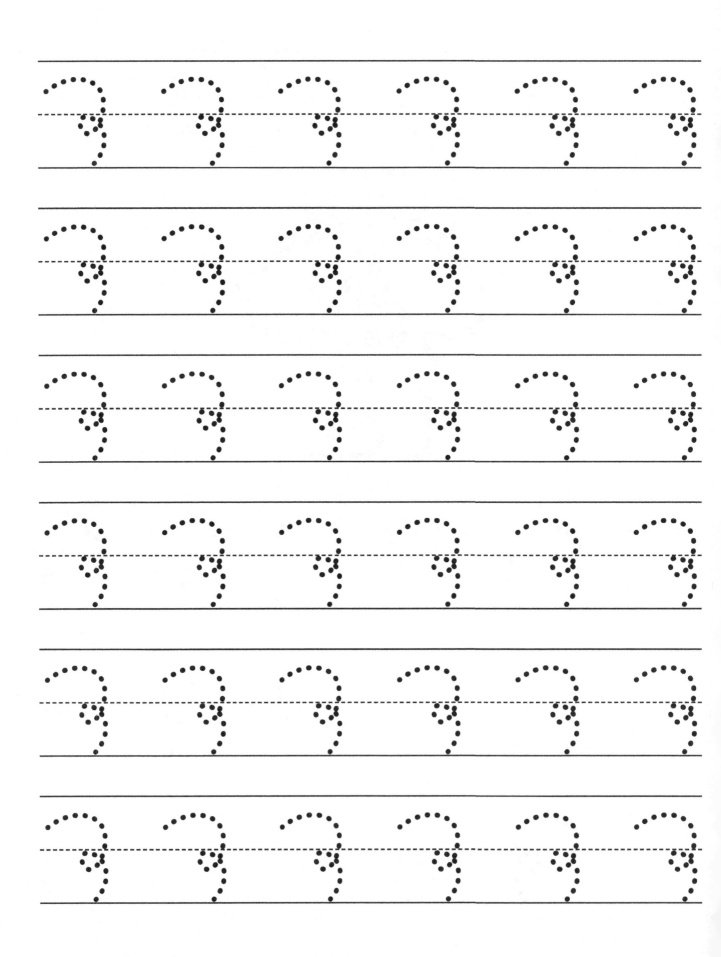

mountain

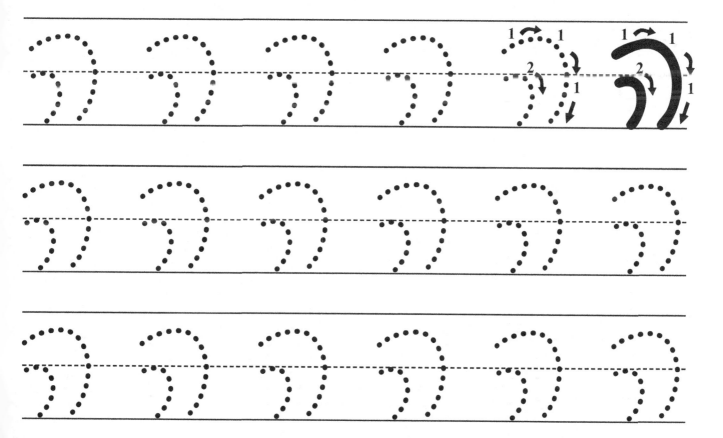

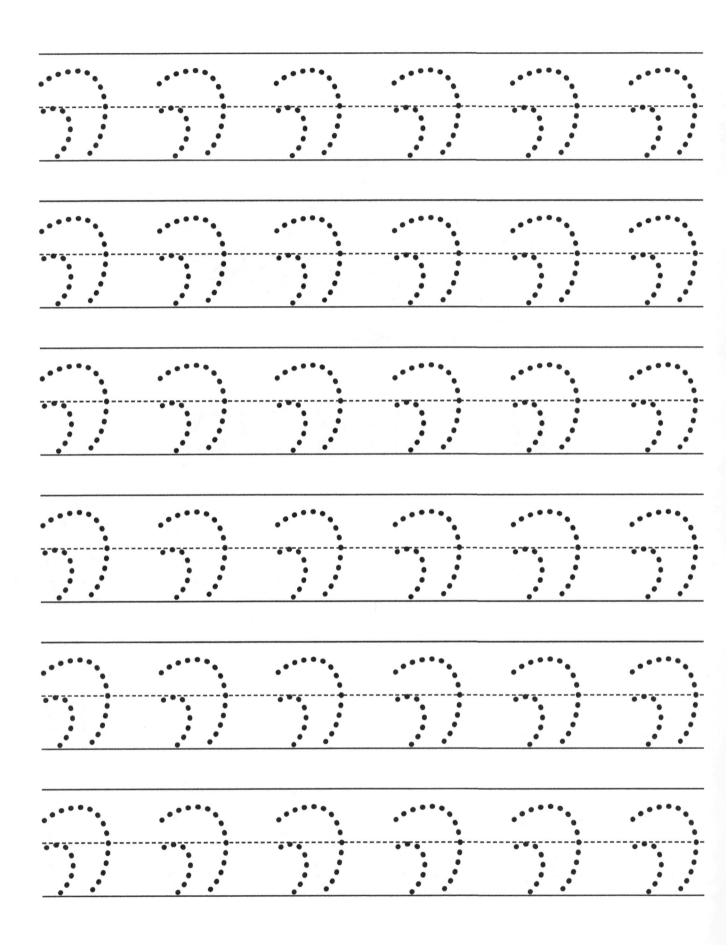

rose

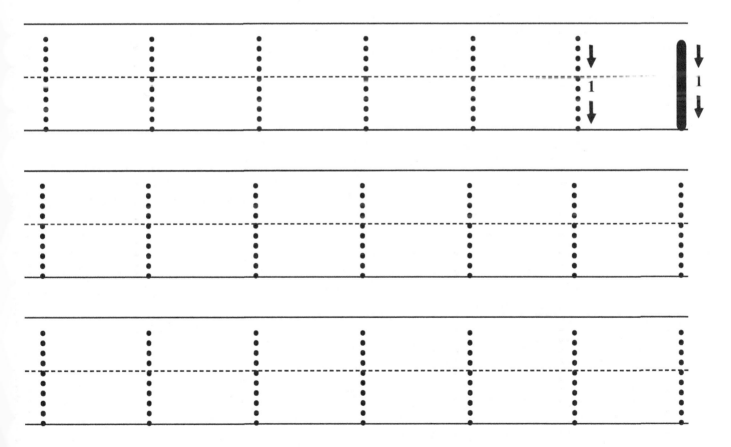

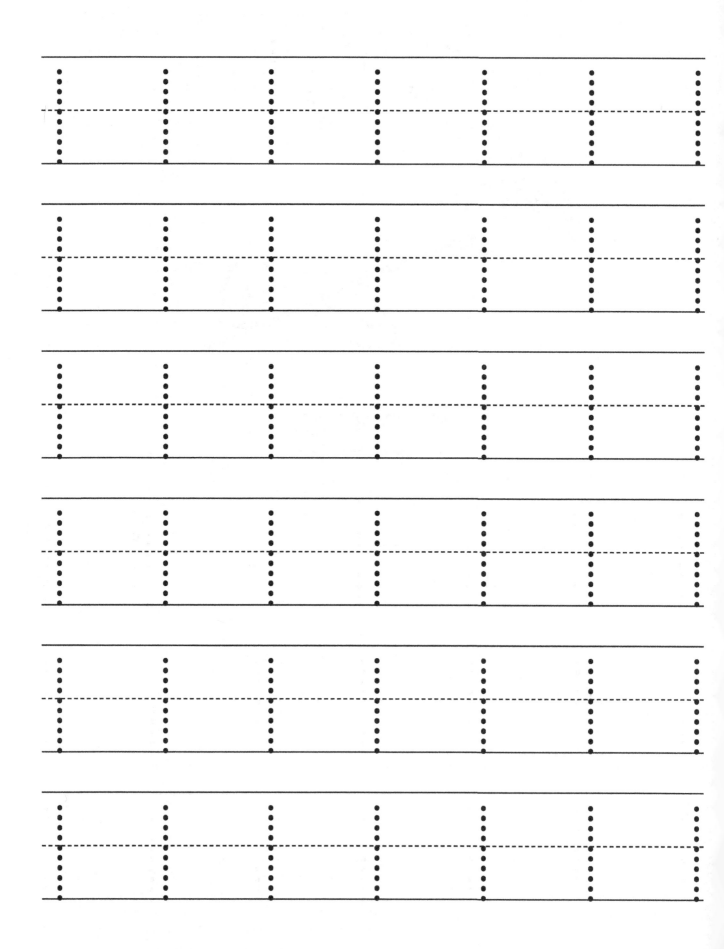

olive

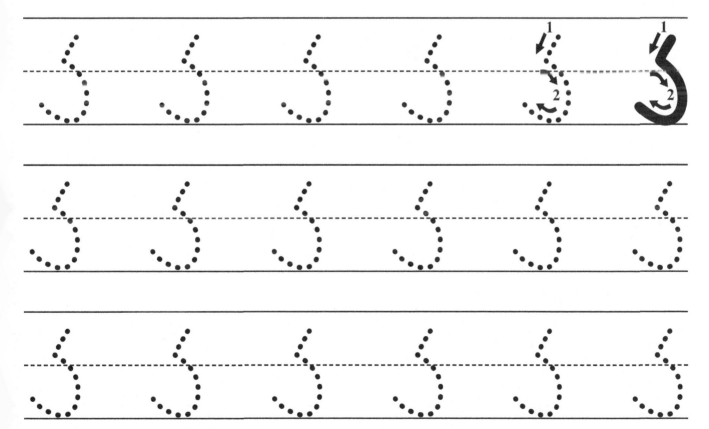

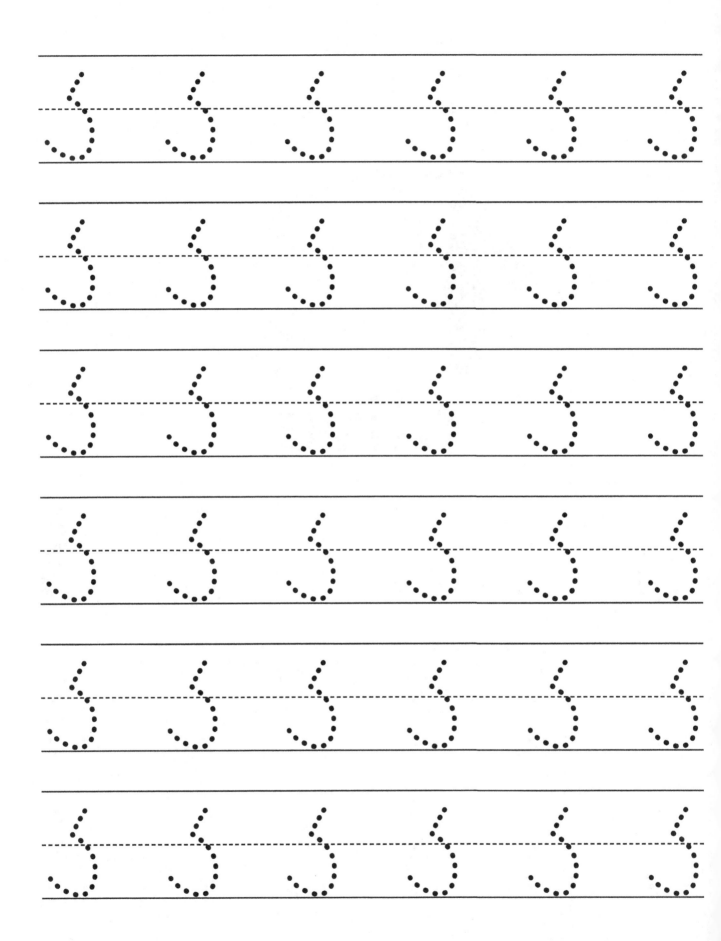

cat

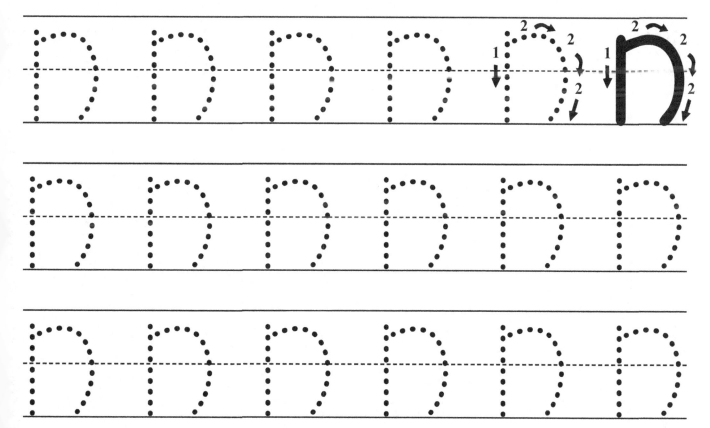

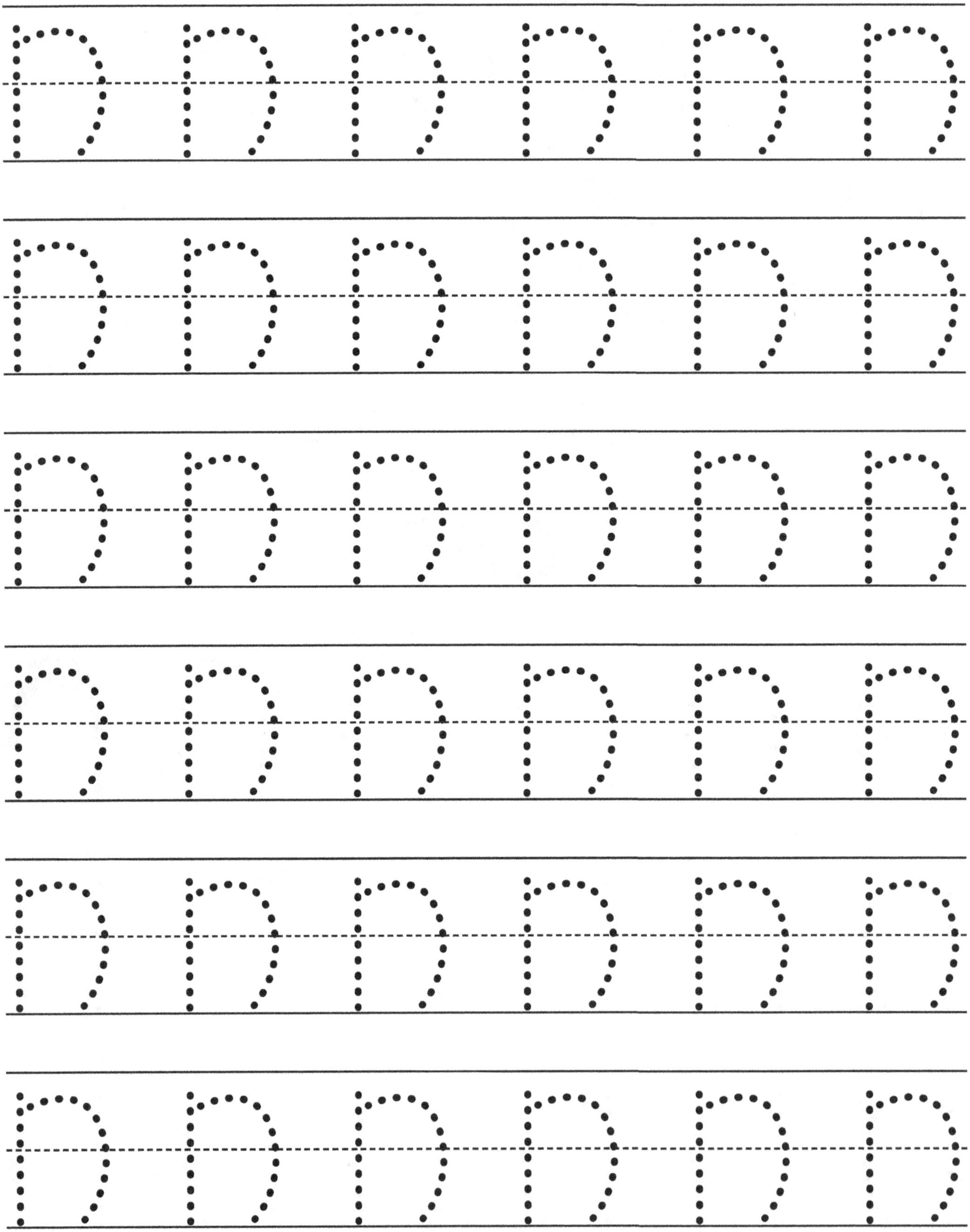

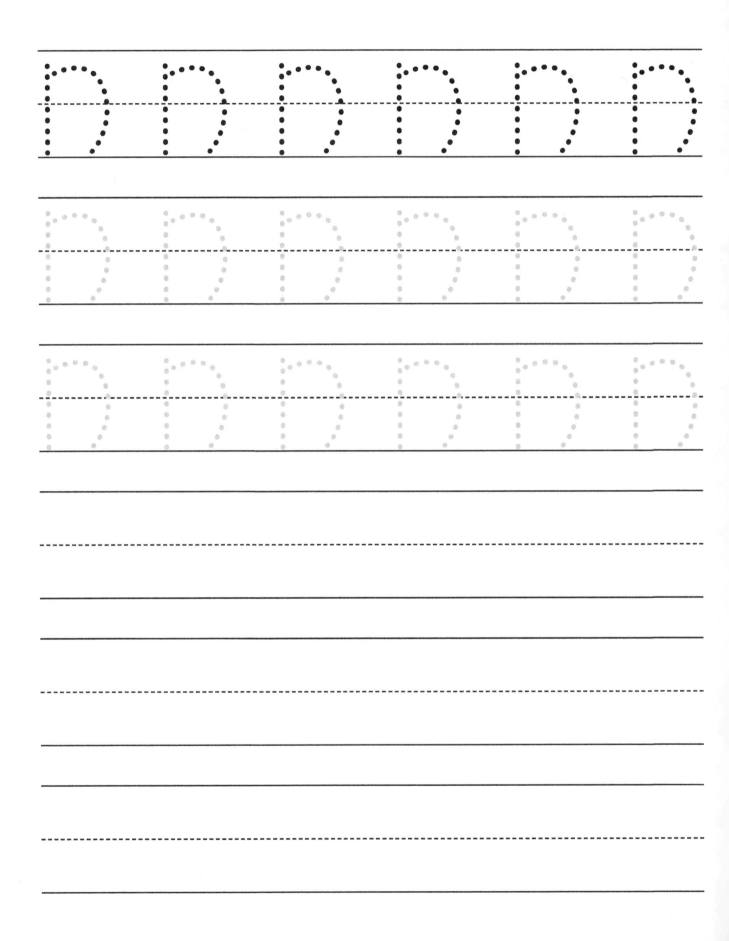

ring

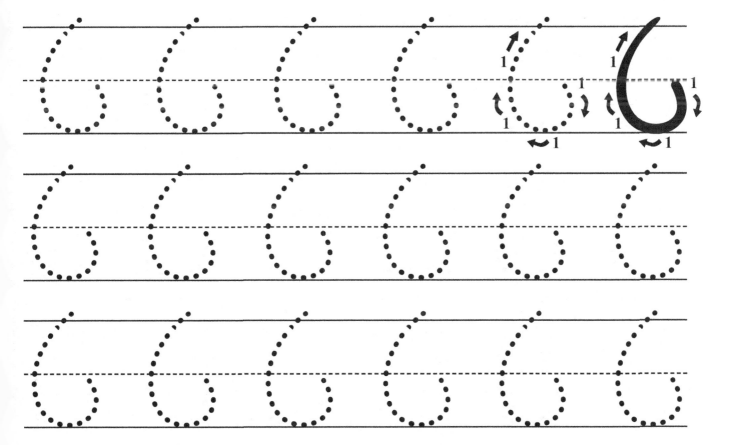

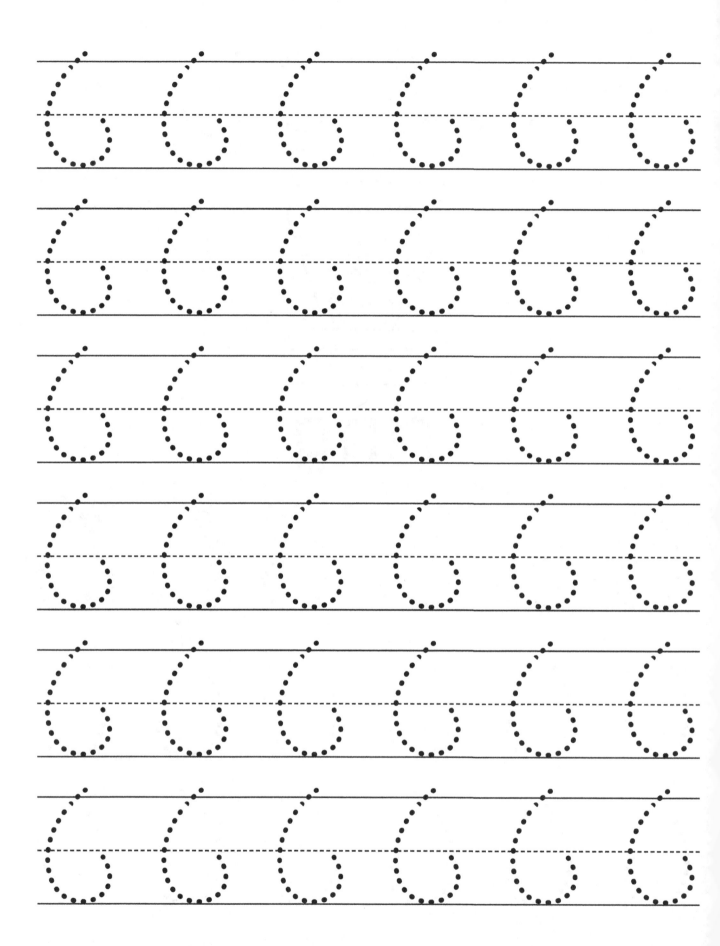

children

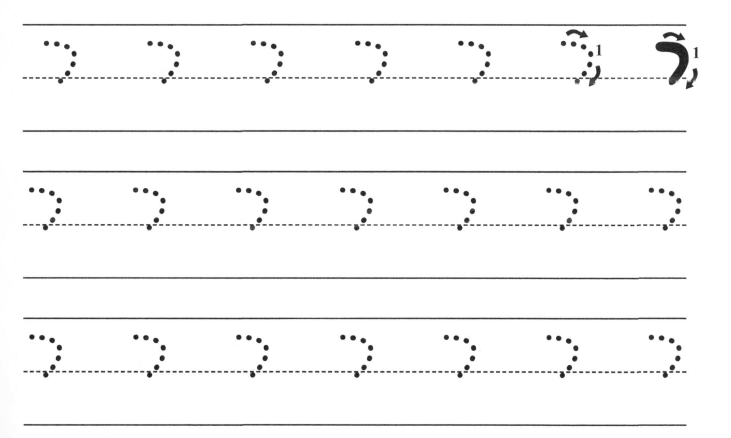

ball

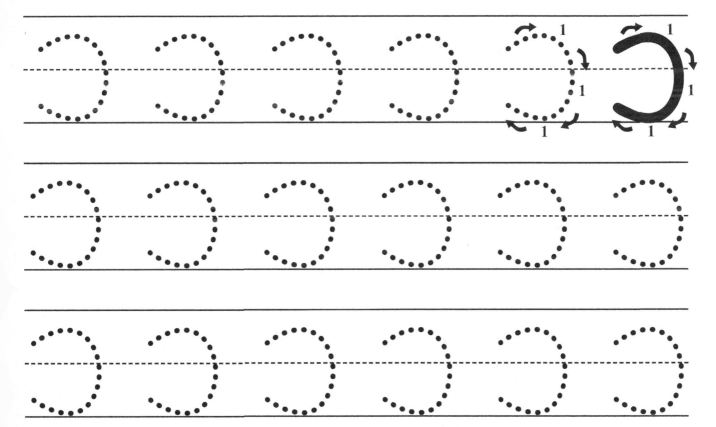

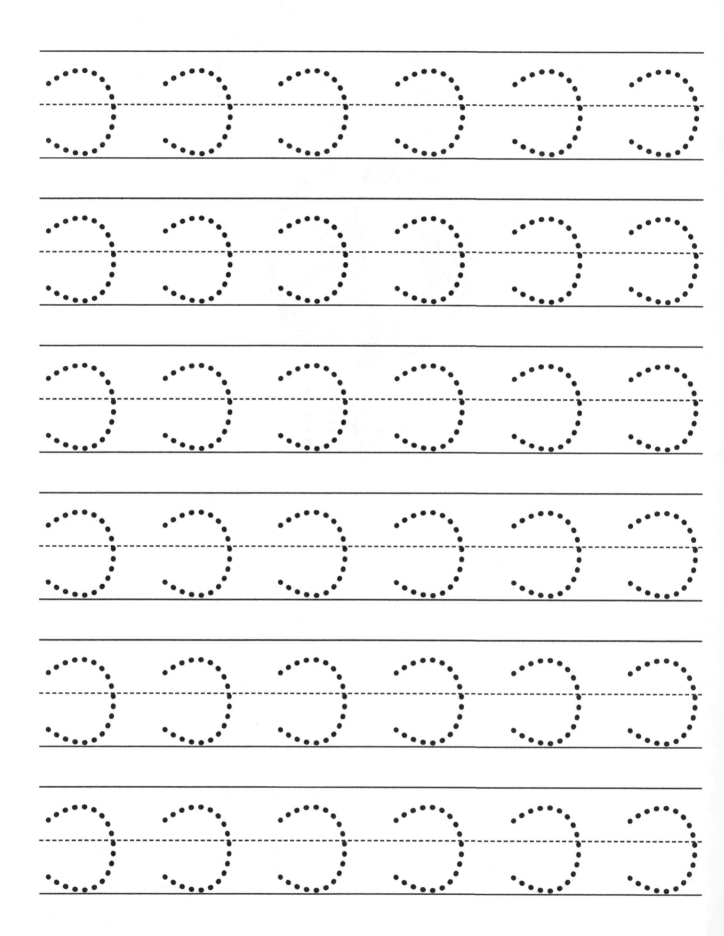

lemon

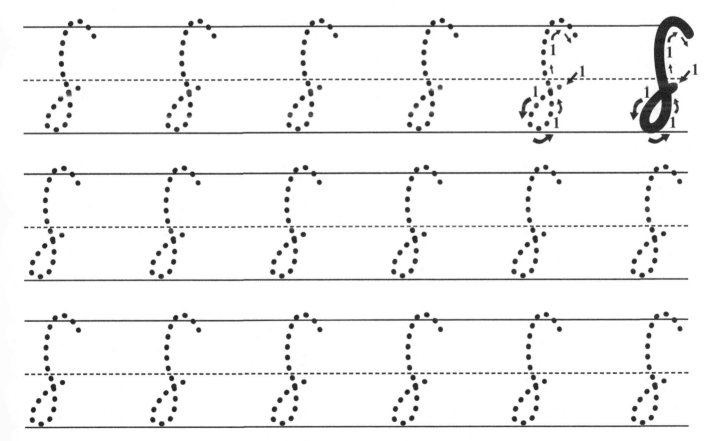

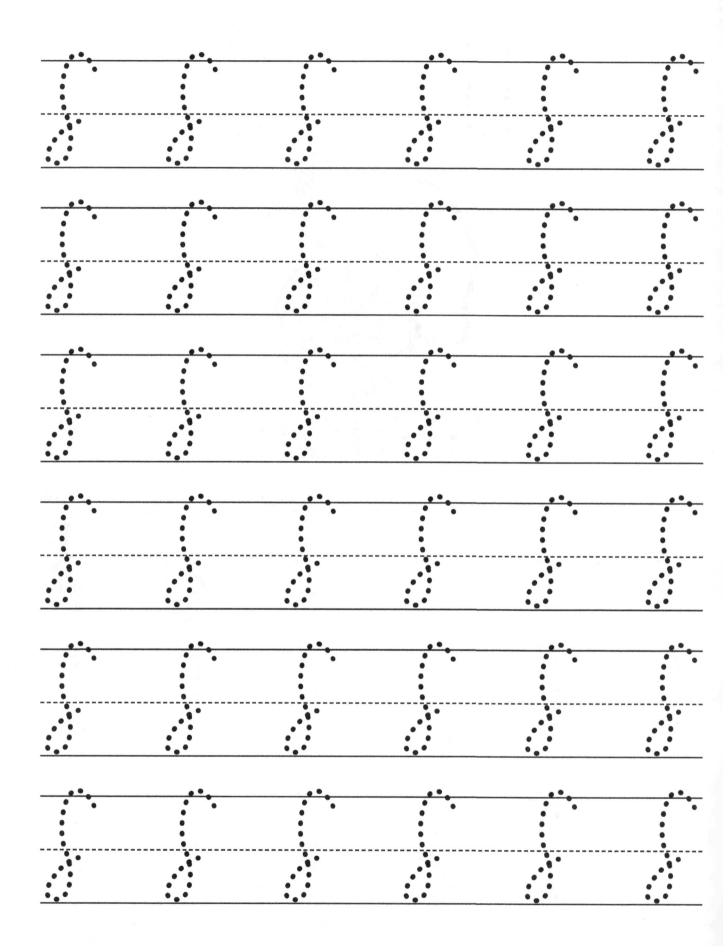

queen

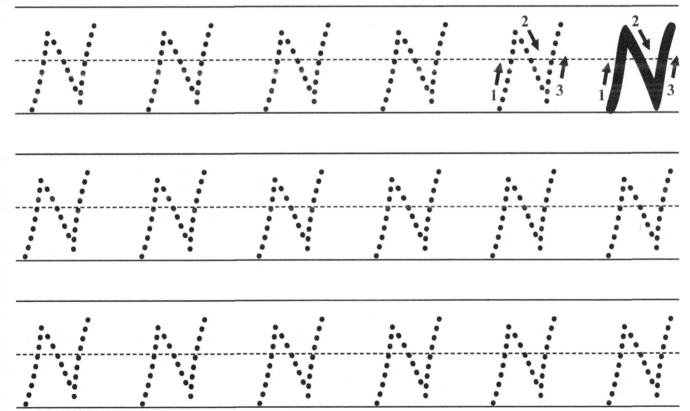

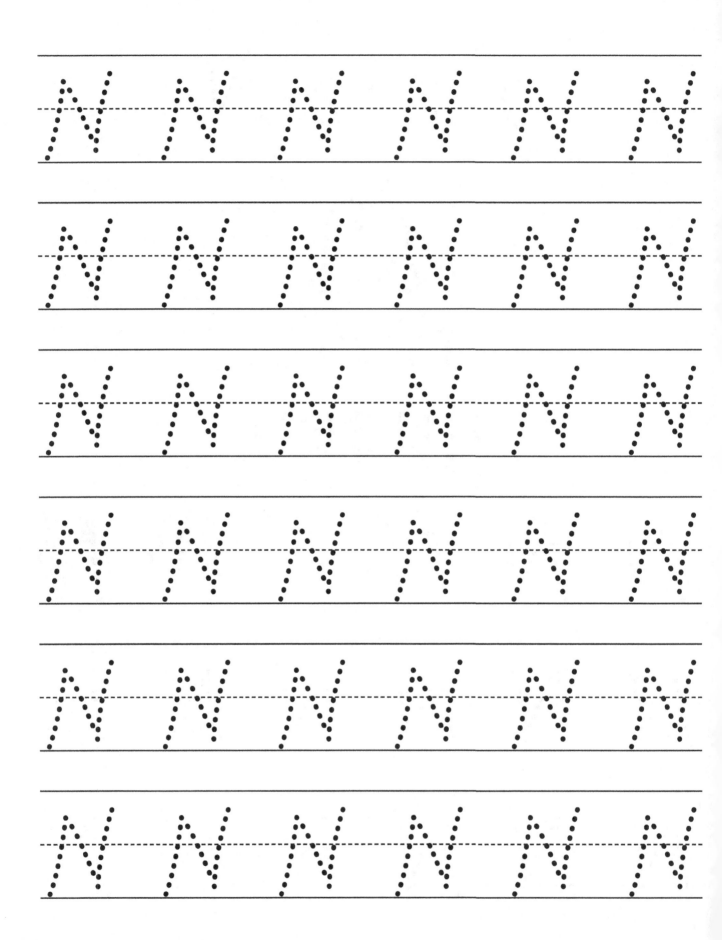

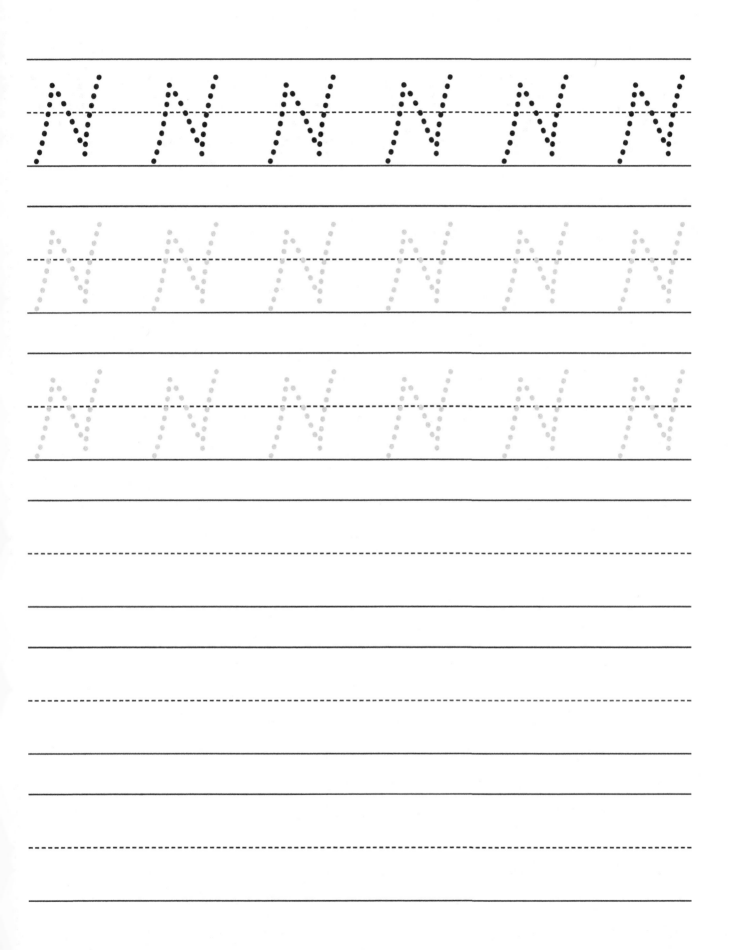

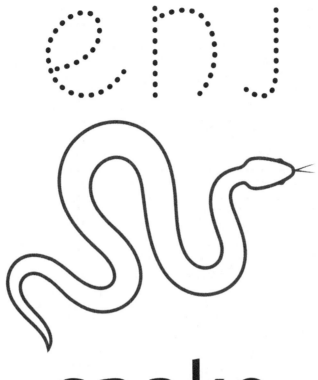

snake

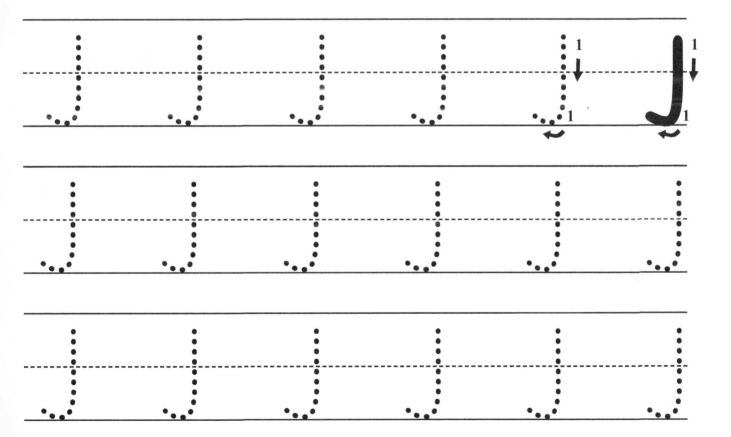

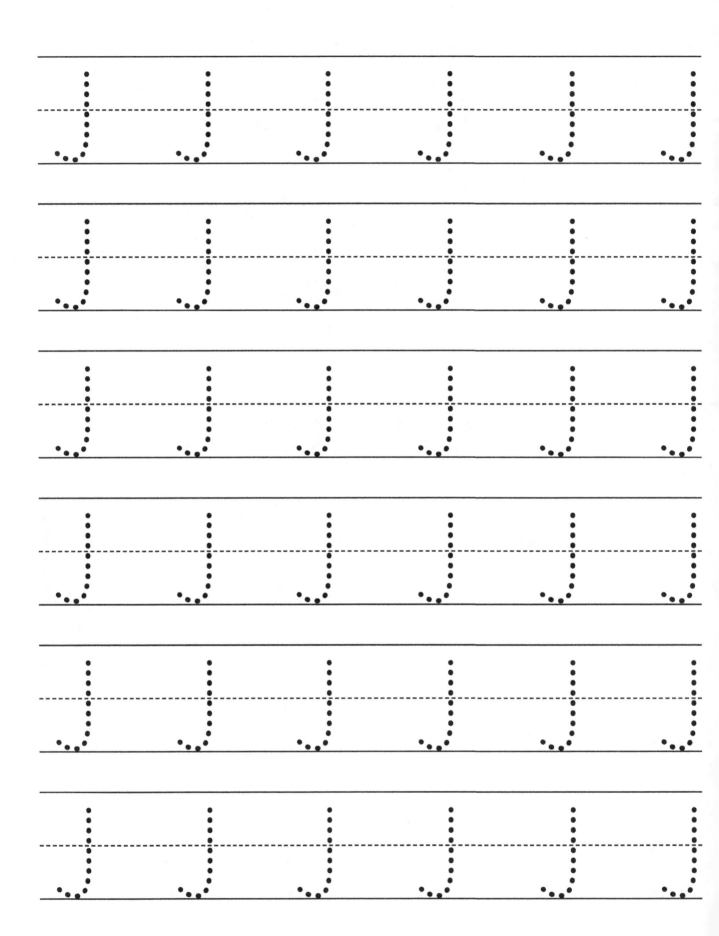

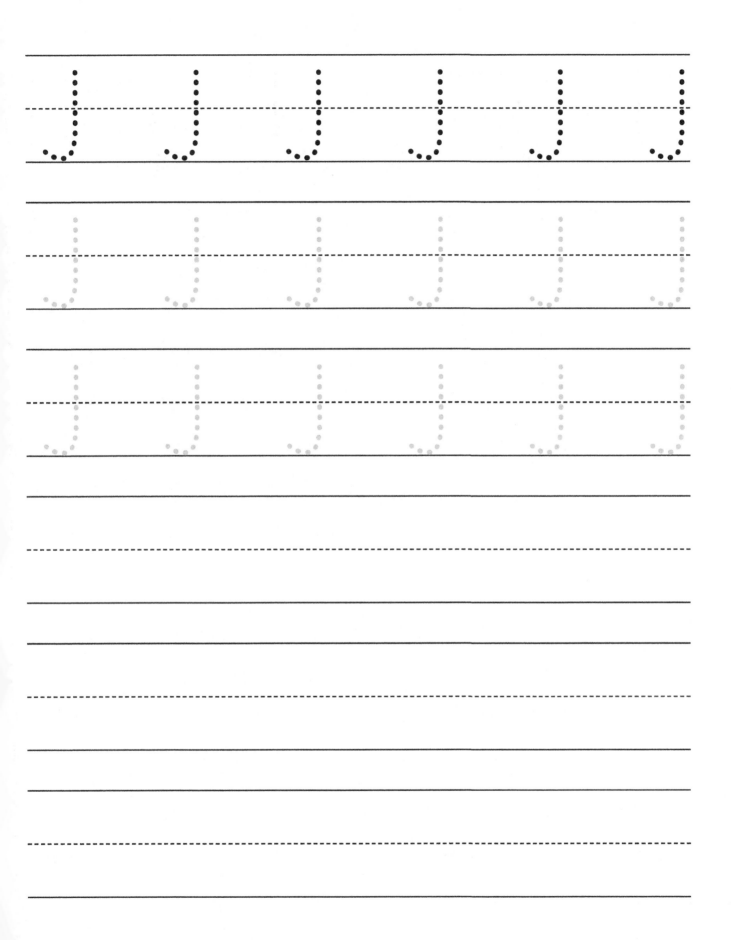

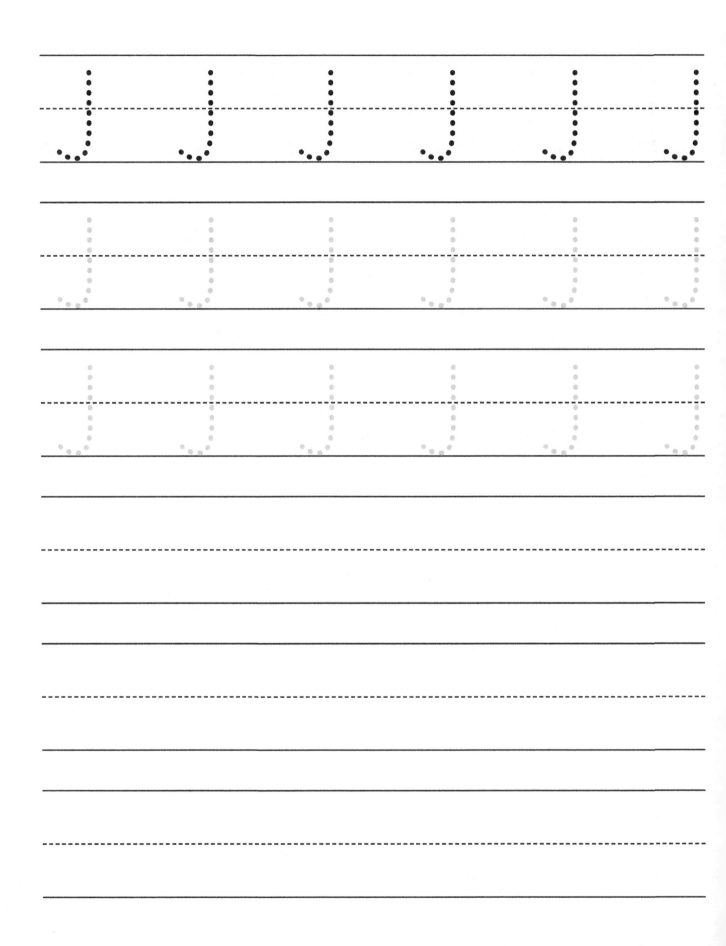

book

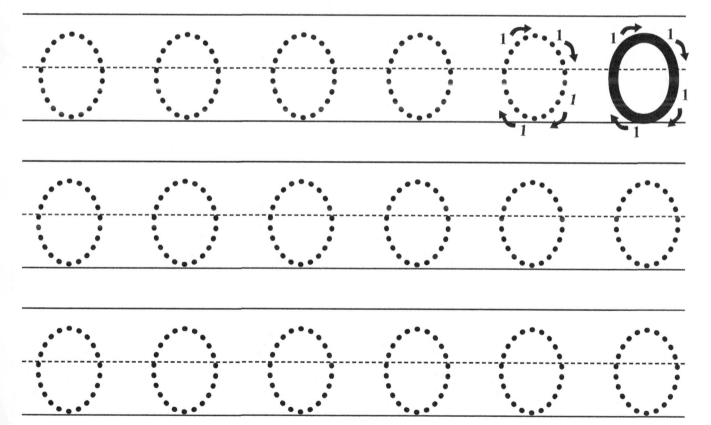

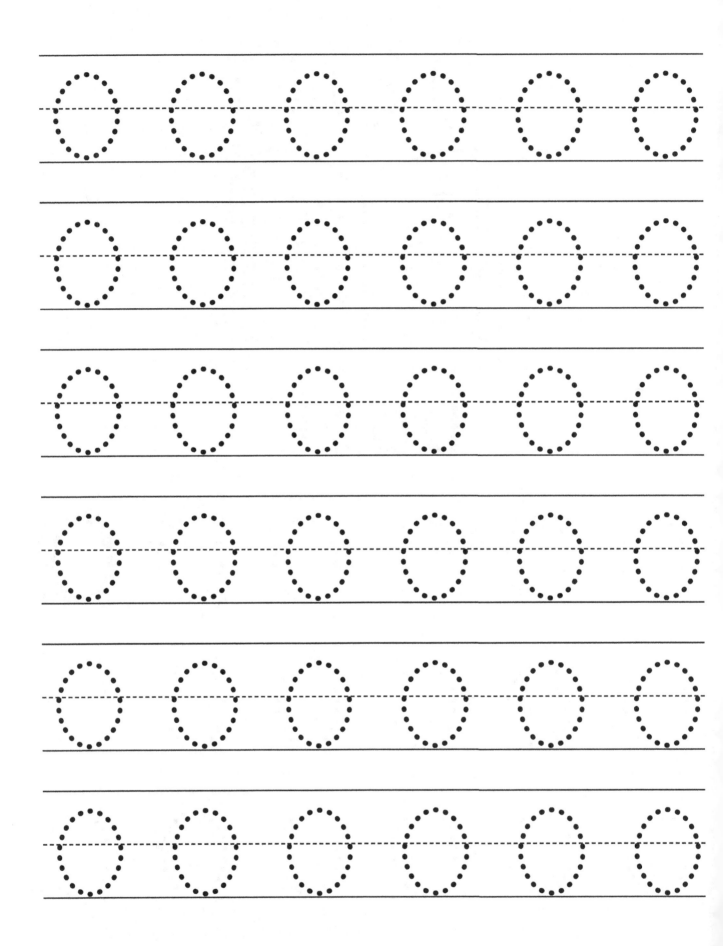

cart

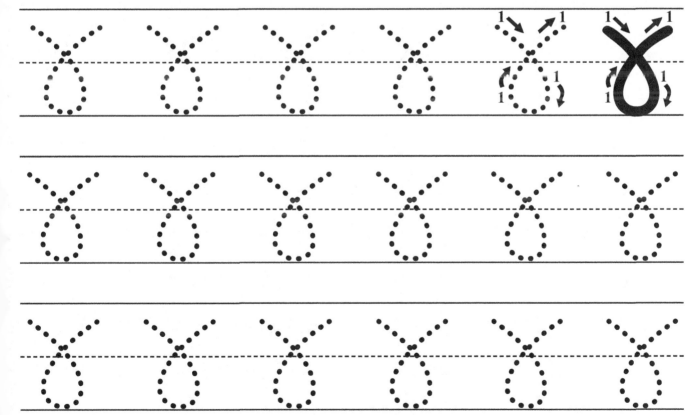

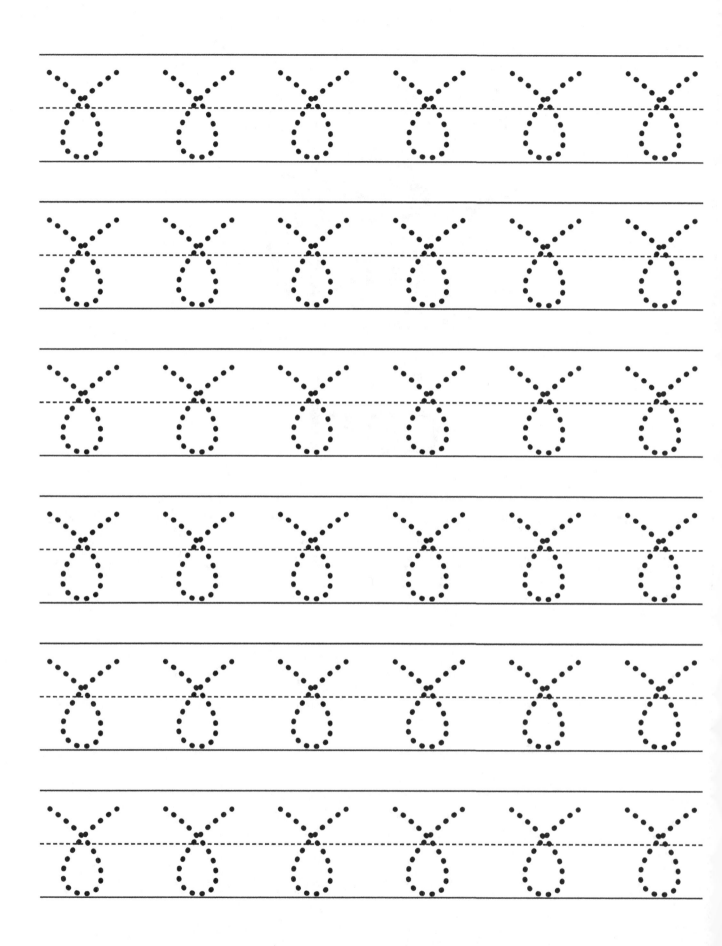

butterfly

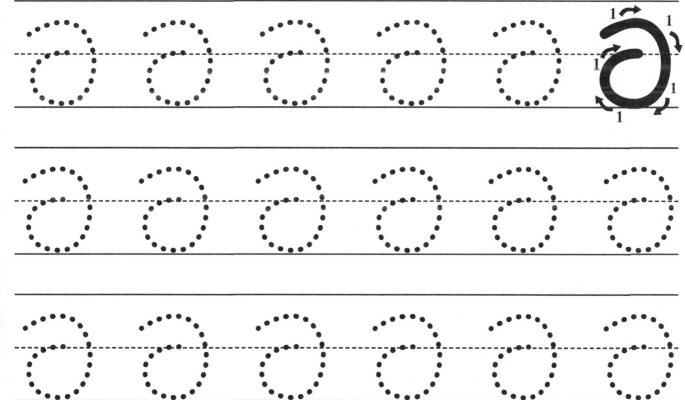

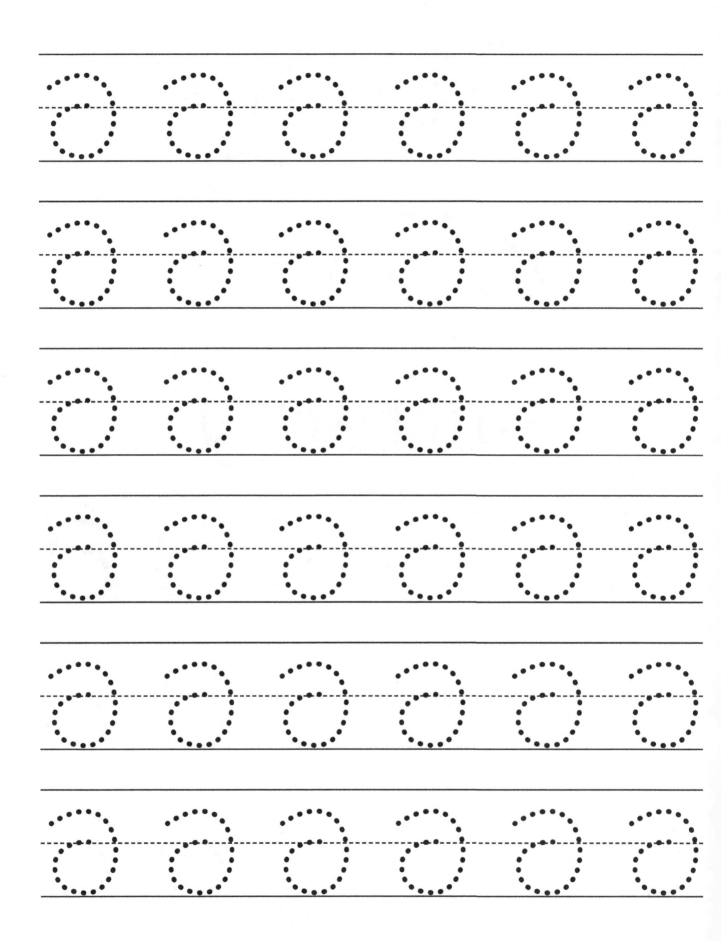

turtle

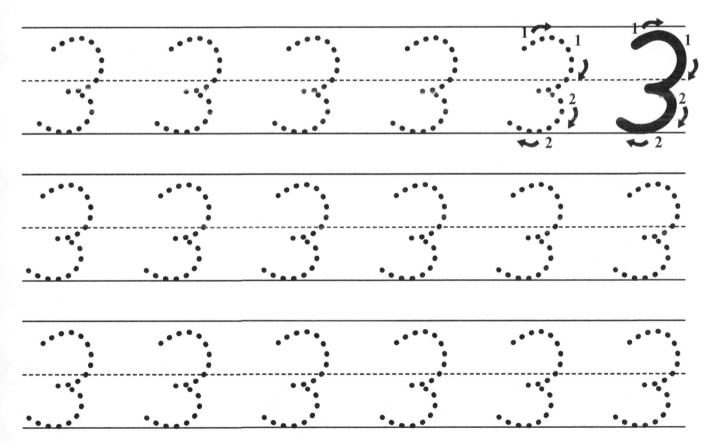

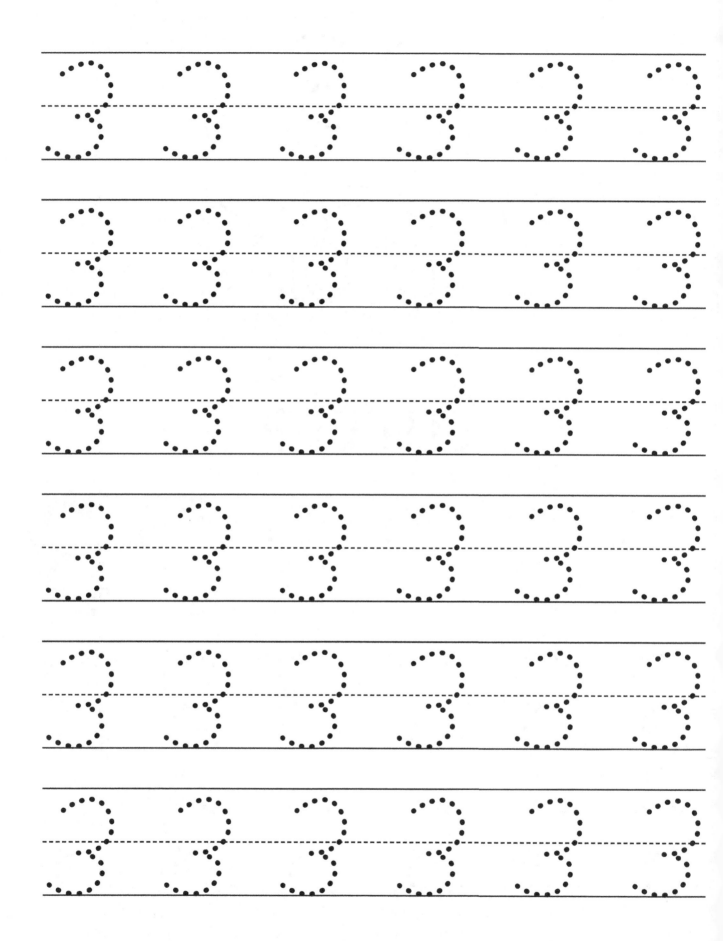

monkey

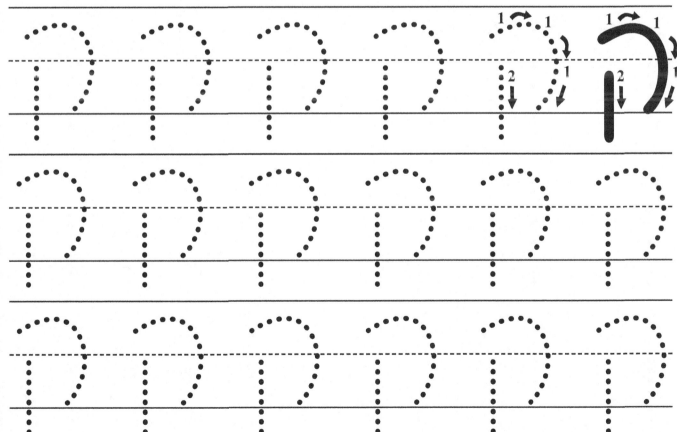

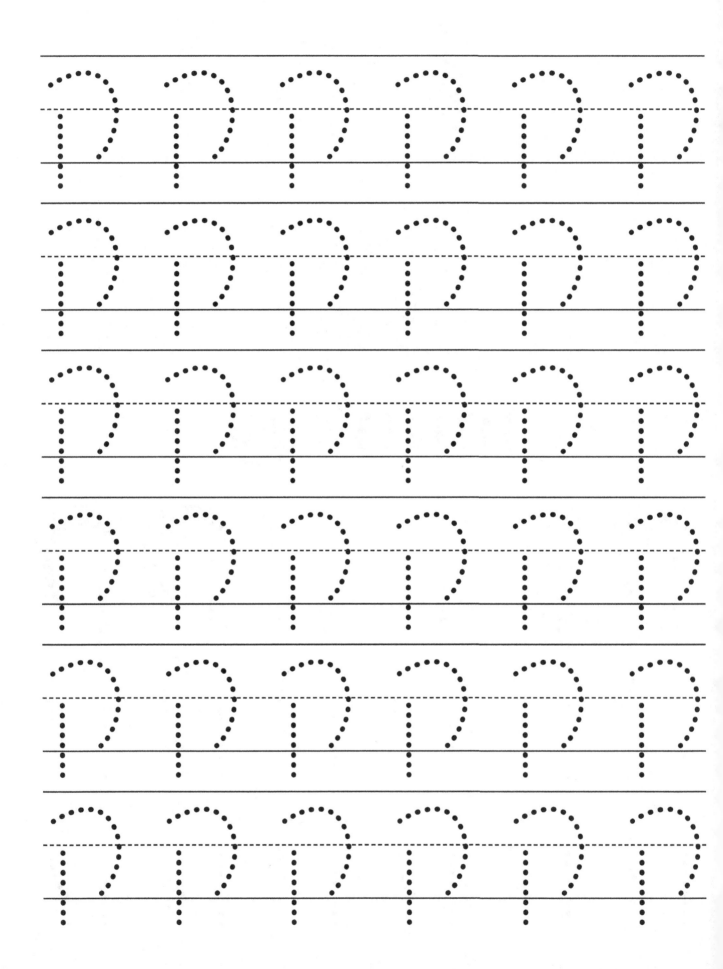

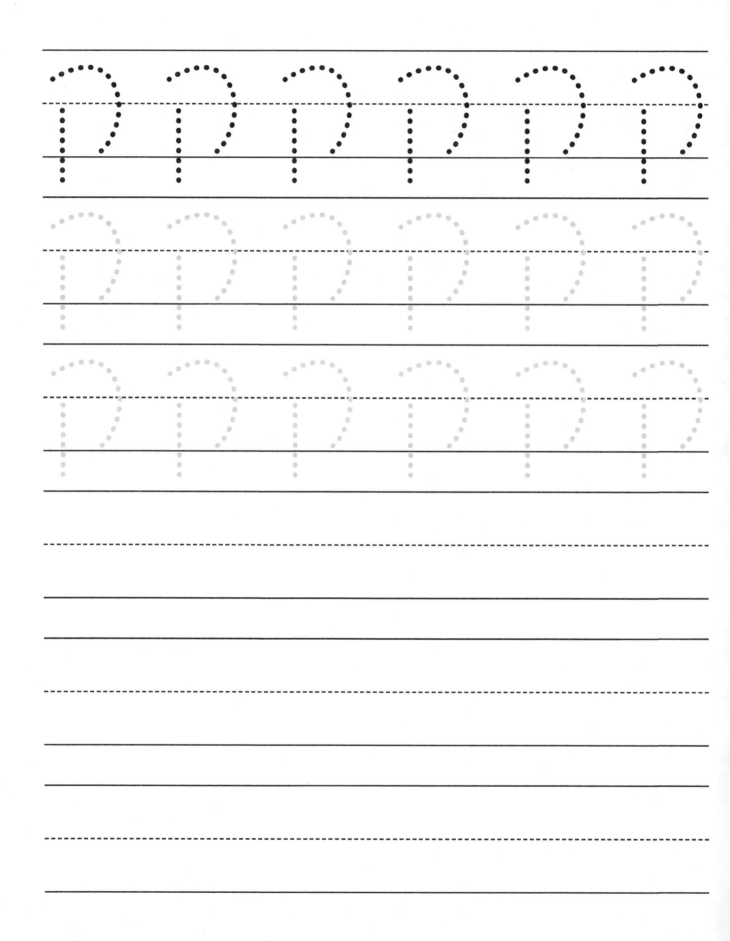

pomegranate

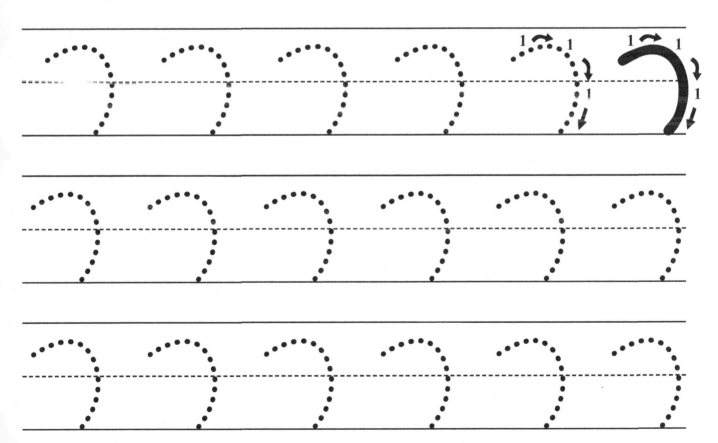

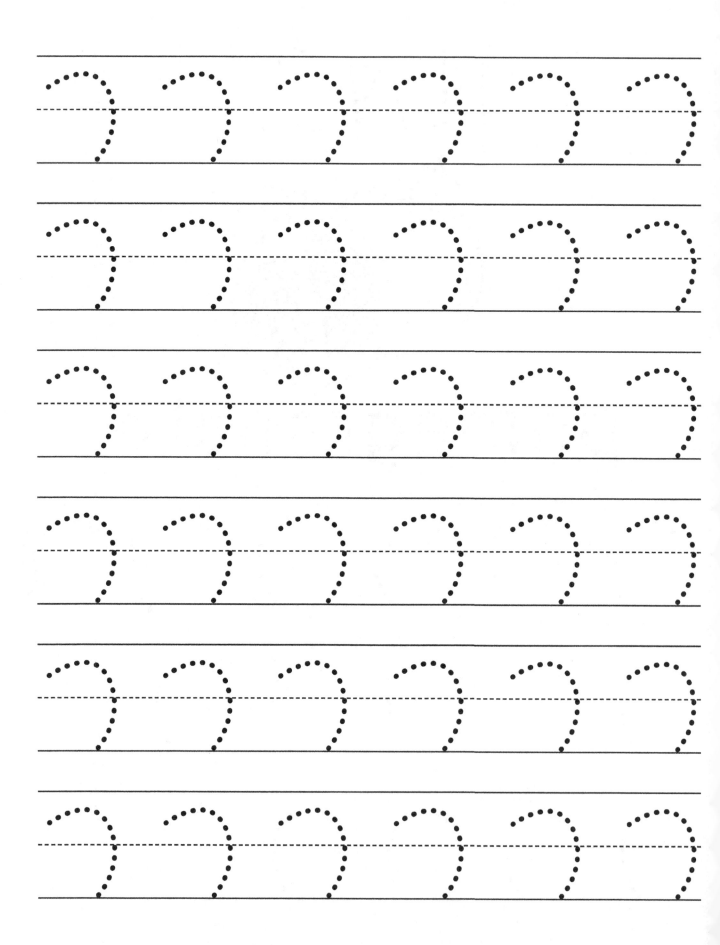

table

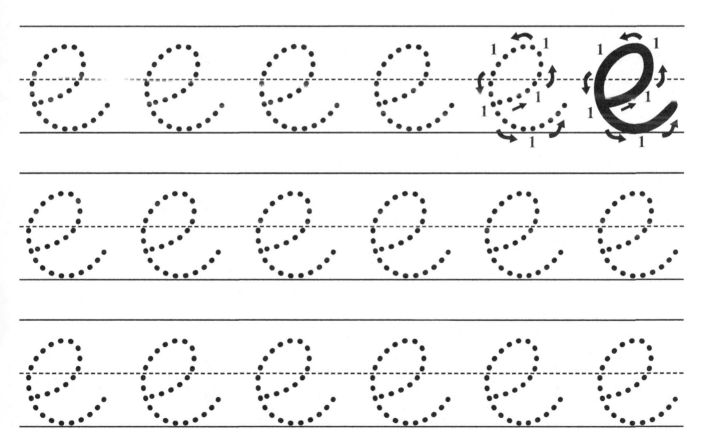

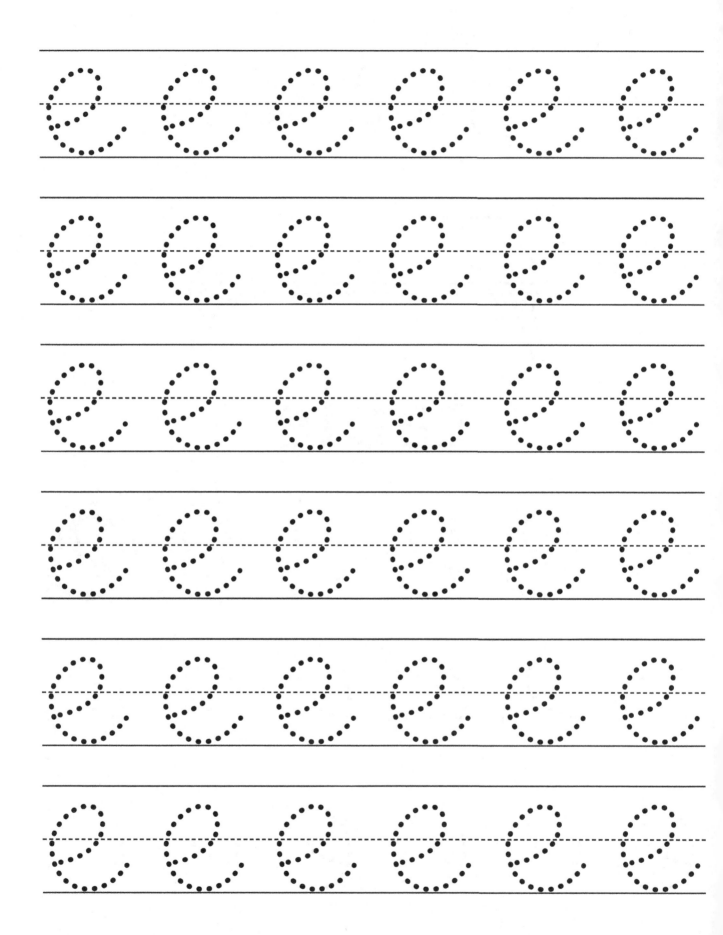

apple

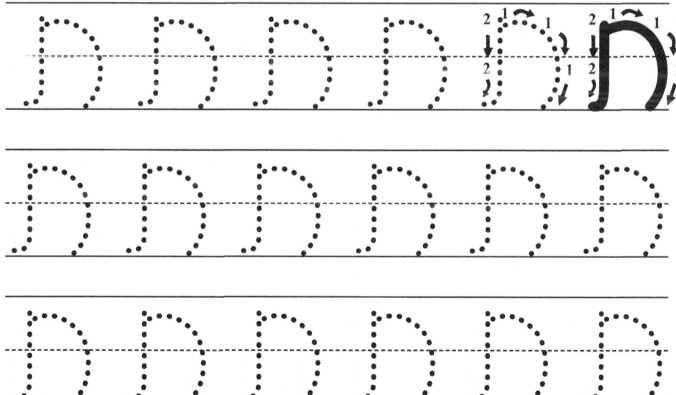

DDDDDD

DDDDDD

DDDDDD

DDDDDD

DDDDDD

DDDDDD

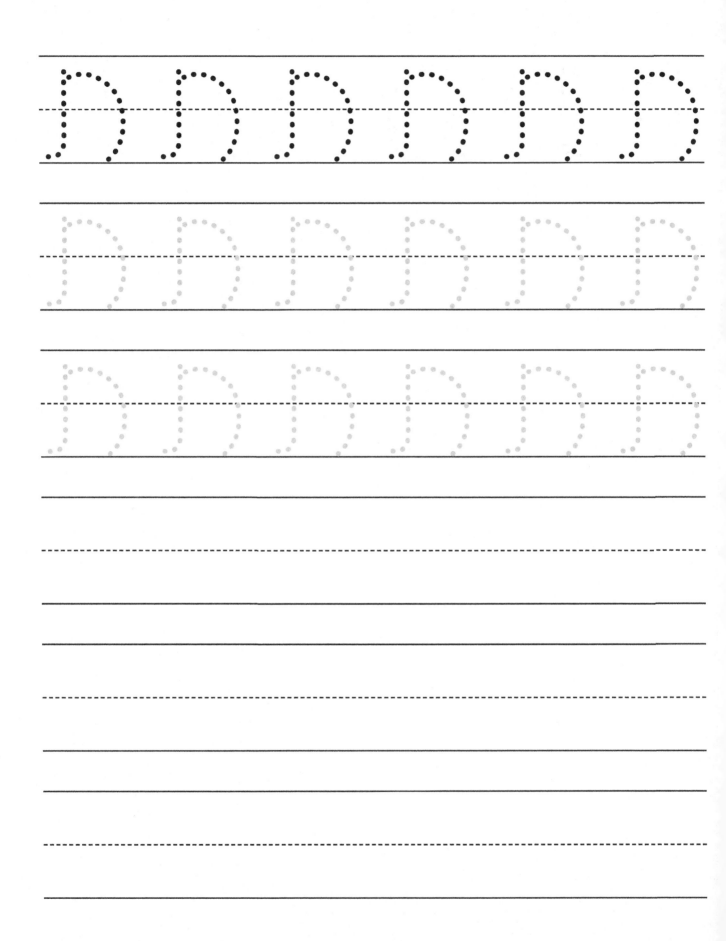

king

water

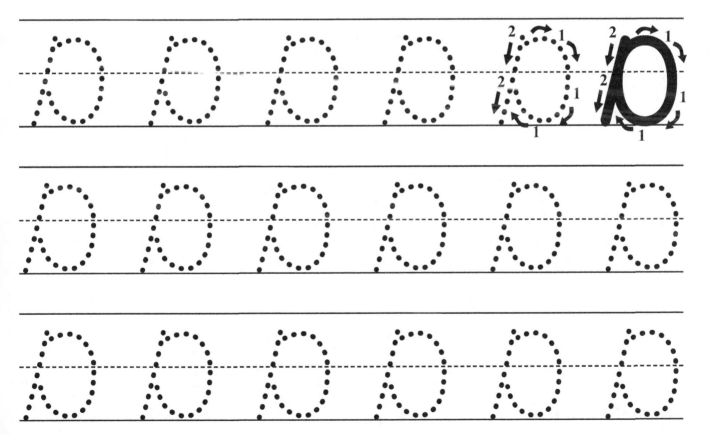

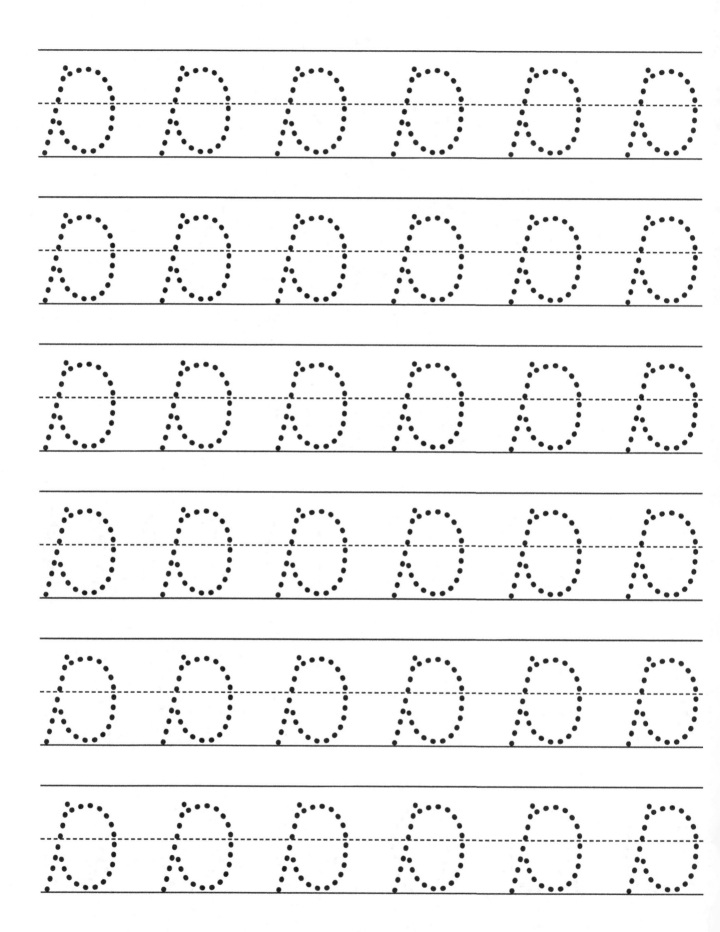

balloon

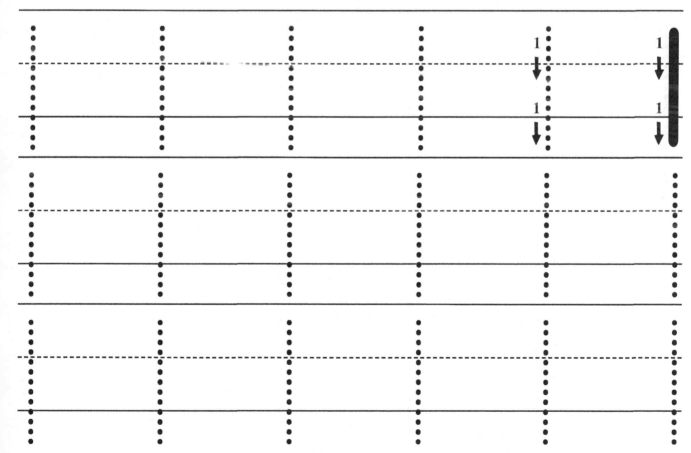

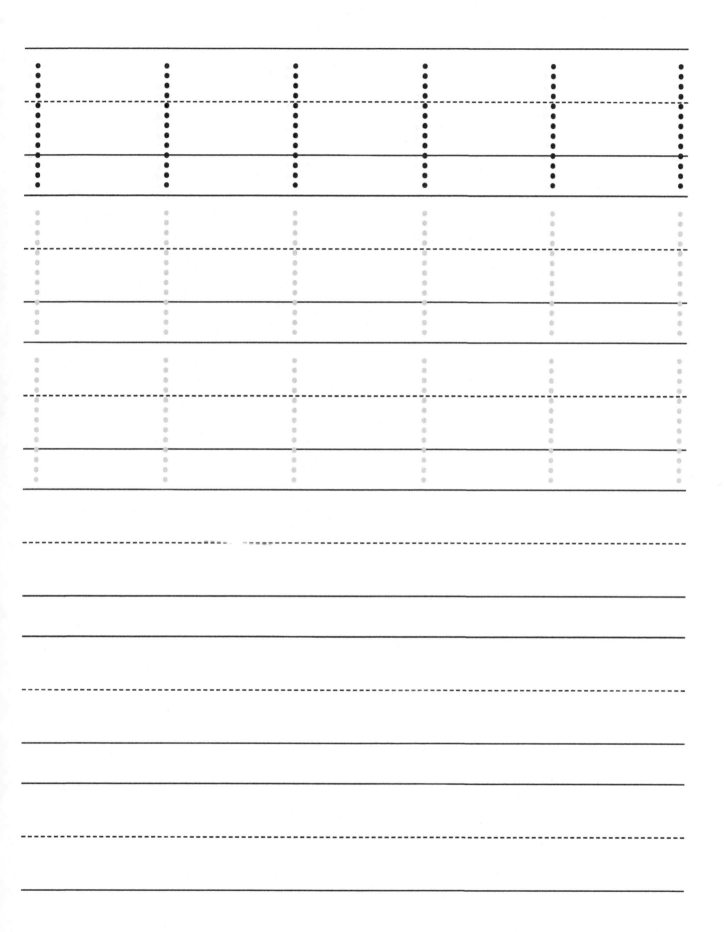

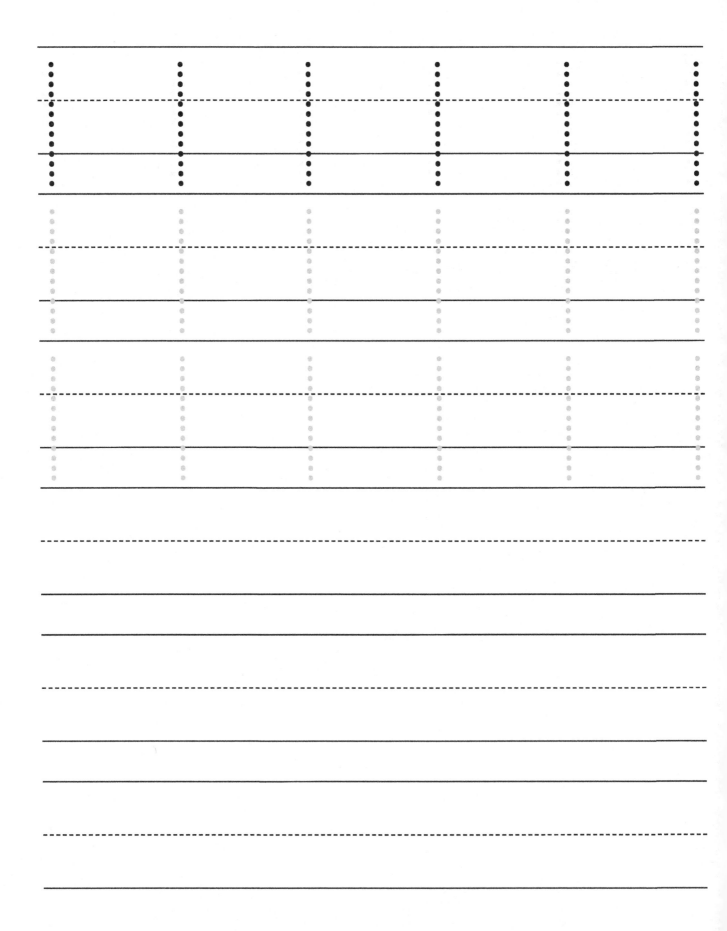

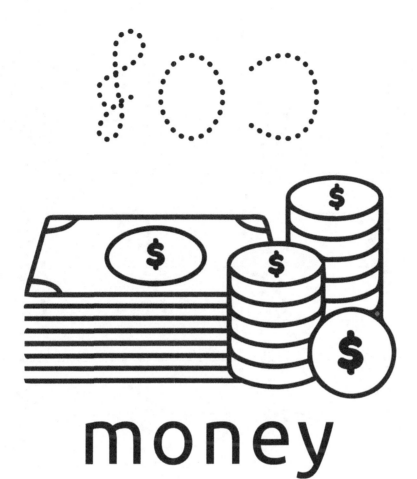

money

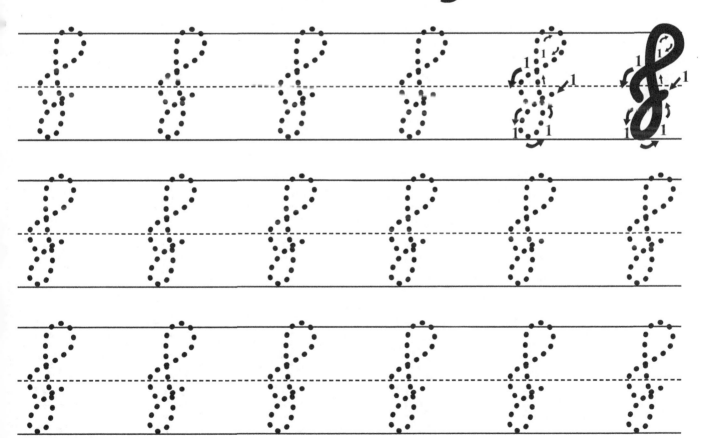

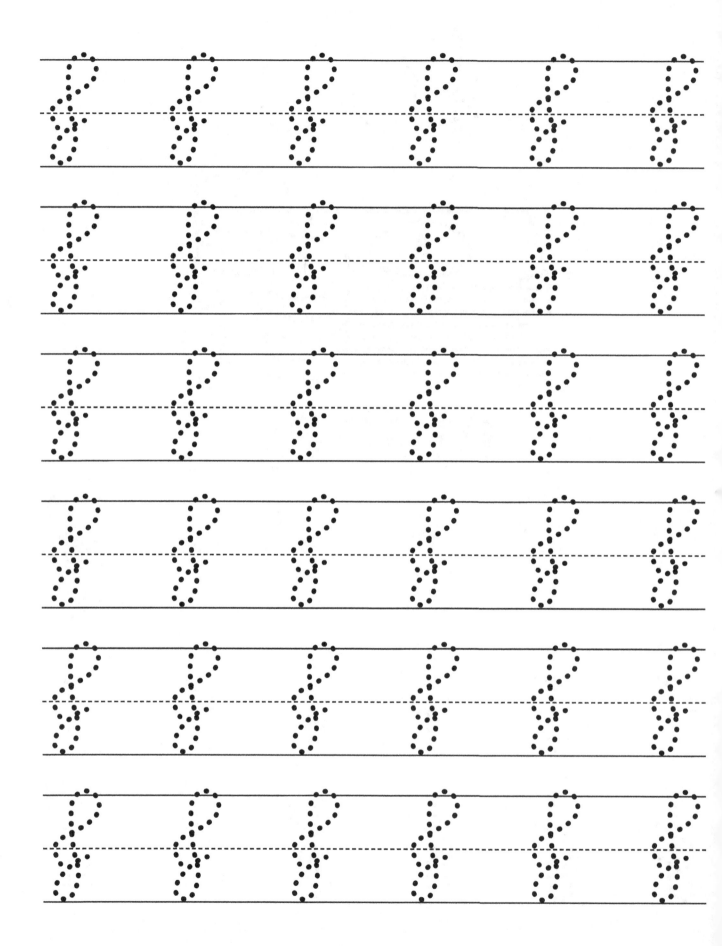

tree

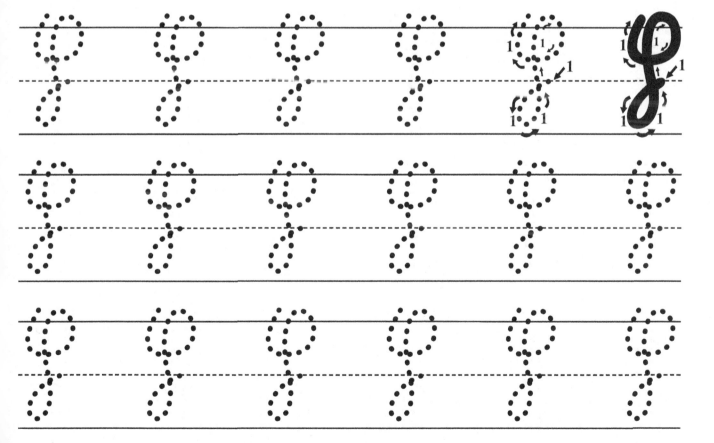

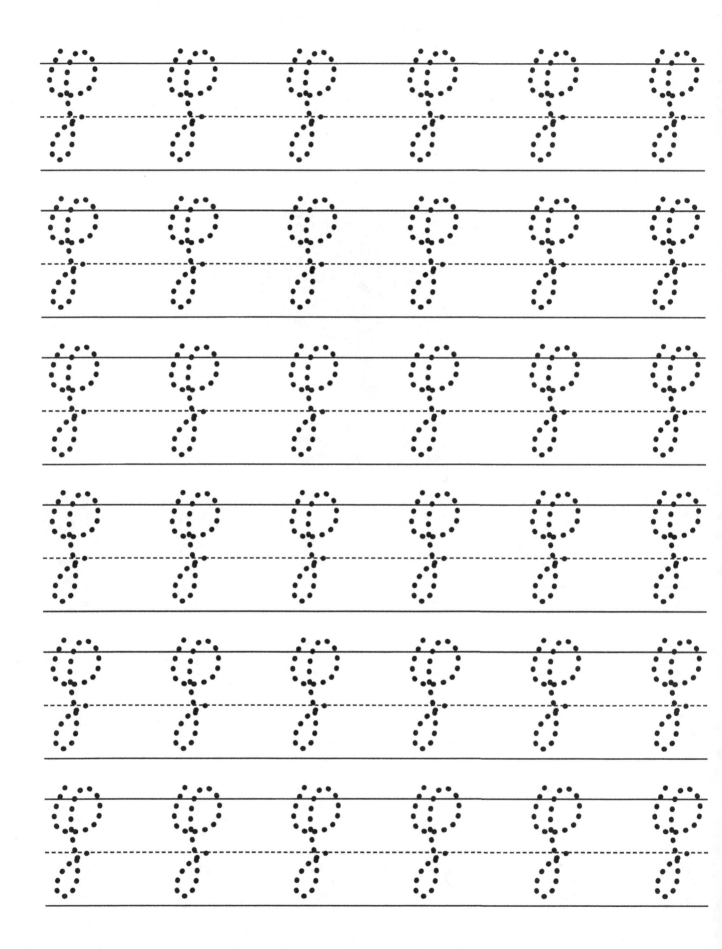

WE WOULD LOVE TO HEAR FROM YOU!
Kindly take a few minutes of your time to leave a
review online at the website you purchased this book!

Made in United States
North Haven, CT
28 May 2024